Spectral Waves

Other Books by Madeline DeFrees

Spectral Waves

New and Uncollected Poems

MADELINE DEFREES

 Copper Canyon Press

Cover art: *Blood Star*, 14" × 11" acrylic on paper, copyright 2002 by Suzanne Stryk

Copper Canyon Press is in residence at Fort Worden State Park in Port Townsend, Washington, under the auspices of Centrum Foundation. Centrum is a gathering place for artists and creative thinkers from around the world, students of all ages and backgrounds, and audiences seeking extraordinary cultural enrichment.

LIBRARY OF CONGRESS CATALOGING-IN-PUBLICATION DATA

DeFrees, Madeline.
Spectral waves: new and uncollected poems / Madeline DeFrees.
    p.   cm.
ISBN 1-55659-240-x (pbk. : alk. paper)
1. Title.
PS3554.E4S67   2006
811'.54 – DC22

                                                            2005031876

9 8 7 6 5 4 3 2   FIRST PRINTING

COPPER CANYON PRESS
Post Office Box 271
Port Townsend, Washington 98368
www.coppercanyonpress.org

for Warren Carrier

ACKNOWLEDGMENTS

Thanks to editors of the following publications in which these poems originally appeared, some in slightly different form:

Atlantic Monthly: "The Visionary under the Knife"

Calyx: "The Music" and "Getting Off" (from "Figures for a Carrousel")

Fragments (Seattle University Magazine): "The Man" and "The Woman" (from "Figures for a Carrousel")

Hubbub: "On My Sixtieth Birthday, I Work at the Yellow Sun," "Time Exposure," and "To a Crow Outside My Bay Window"

Hyperion: A Poetry Journal, Black Sun, New Moon (Special Women's Issue): "The Ride" and "The Child" (from "Figures for a Carrousel")

Image: A Journal of the Arts & Religion: "The Poetry of Eyes," "The Eye," "An Elegy for Dan," "Lodestar," and "*The Magdalen with the Nightlight* by Georges de La Tour"

Indiana Review: "Serpentine Soliloquy"

Massachusetts Review: "The scissor-tailed swallow" and "Paula Executes the Angels"

New Letters: "*Dressing the Dead Girl* by Gustave Courbet," "Synthesizing Spider Silk," and "To a Former Lover in His Sanctuary"

North Dakota Quarterly: "*After great pain, a formal feeling comes*"

Northwest Review: "The Family Group" (from "Figures for a Carrousel"); also included in *When Sky Lets Go* (New York: George Braziller, 1978) and in *Blue Dusk: New & Selected Poems* (Port Townsend: Copper Canyon Press, 2001)

Puerto del Sol: "Smokehouse Blues"

River City: "A Crown of Sonnets for 'The King'"

Southern Review: "The Poetry of Swans" and "The Spider in *Brewer's Dictionary*"

Yale Review: "Broken Sleep"

Special thanks to Patricia Solon, who generously volunteered her expert computer skills, and to Michael Harper for his suggestions.

Finally, thanks to the friends who read the manuscript or individual poems: Thomas Aslin, Warren Carrier, Jennifer Maier, Anne McDuffie, Lia Purpura, Patricia Solon, and Joan Swift, and to Keith Funai, Rory McGowan, and Eric Miyake for help with the author photo.

Contents

Spectral Waves

One

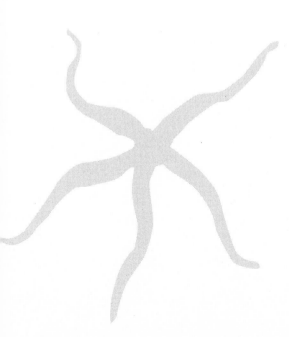

The Poetry of Eyes

In a dark time, Roethke writes,
the eye begins to see. But only with the heart.
The history of eyes, like their anomalies,
is written on the retina, in every image stored
and every stunning line of record.
Bogan's ambition: *A passion wholly of the mind,*
Thought divorced from eye

                    and bone. The eye as horseman
passes by Yeats's limestone epitaph,
casts *a cold eye / On Life, on death*, and knows not why
faith strikes a bargain with the Tyger
burning in Blake's song, its *fearful symmetry*
framed by *immortal hand or eye*.
God, too, burns bright in the Burning Bush

whose downward rush of flame demands a dimming of
the glare with filmy veils of gossamer;
that is, *goose summer* or even *God's summer*—a spell
of fine weather in late fall. The fragile
cloth of Mary's winding-sheet as she goes back
to Heaven, and we celebrate our newfound vision:
the Indian summer of the eye.

Smokehouse Blues

for Joan Swift

The bluebird of happiness, once in a blue moon,
camps on your doorjamb. In the tribal
smokehouse, ash filters down onto the back of your
black sweater, reclaims the natural
gray of your blond hair. What are you doing here,
you a founding member of CAWF,
the acronym for Citizens Against Woodstove
Fumes?

       Under a humanoid stove, duking it out, your
slogan reads: *Give your lungs a fighting chance.*
No wonder I wince, retracing that blue
legend, the breath of fire on your blue jeans.
The night we drove to dinner flaunting your bumper
sticker, a man rolled down his car window
and shouted: *Where can I get a sticker like that?*

Blue eyes ecstatic, you smiled back. Inside Ray's
Boathouse, you disappeared, as you always do,
into the *Ladies* to check your lipstick, your hair.
It was blue Monday. I memorized the menu,
the waiter hovering. When you stayed away too long
I knew you were on the prowl for the man who
coveted your CAWF. For thirty years, you've been
the Allergy Queen

       of Edmonds. Now you're turning
blue in the bleachers. And I worry, my true-blue
friend, headed for another cardiac

arrest, this could bring on the end, your flight
with the Blue Angels. I'm reviewing procedures
for CPR when the star of the show winds down.
One poet staggers out, feeling, he says,
like a smoked ham. But you are a sacrificial lamb.
It's a Blue Ribbon performance.

The Eye

Lodged in a bony orbit in the skull, the eye
is slower than the hand
and more inclined to doubt in spite of
what the old saw claims: *Seeing is believing*.
This was not the case with skeptic
Thomas, who put his unbelieving hand
into the Master's wounded side

                        and only then
declared his faith. I trust the eye; it winnows
wheat from chaff. And in the furnace, separates
true metal from slag. An eye for minimal
upheaval proves a mode of second
sight: the anthill army's small
earthmoving crew. Wrought-iron handrails

filigreed with spider-cloth, sequined with dew.
Half-open clematis against
a chain-link fence, their creamy lemon
shading into white. Blue-black sky
swept clean with brushwork in the evening
light and winter-bare japonica's faint
flush of green before the leaves come out.

Because the eyes are windows on the soul, wise
men close the curtain. Hoard rivers of bright
color. When words arrive with hearts
pinned to their sleeve, the brave will plunge
the writing hand into the right-brain
wound to draw out blood and water
the doubter can believe.

Broken Sleep

Three times a night, I climb from my Percocet
dream—the repetitive reel of
falling—drawn by a flashlight beam into my cold
Wake Island kitchen where comfort
waits in a small white

                         tablet that throws open
the gates of horn and ivory. In bed I feel
barrel staves tighten
around my chest. This is the year the ravening
beast, locked in my rib cage,

                        breaks free,
stalks the sad moonscape meant to leave me
with one bulletproof breast: a dental
patient weighed down by the lead in an X-ray
vest. The dream is always

                        the same: blueberry
bush in its bird-netting sash at the rockery
crown. The animal cry piercing
the hush. Stones taking aim at the flung
body parts plummeting down to collect
in a heap on the sidewalk.

Naming the Cataracts

If my doctor had told me, *You have stars in your eyes,*
the line more than a metaphor of
young love; or if *seeing stars* meant something other
than being knocked out cold,
how could the feelings of old age be hurt by a diagnosis
of cataracts? Language is everything.
I know that I saw stars whenever I
walked into sun, or when oncoming cars
blinded me with headlights.

      How often I'm drawn into
danger by mirage. Bold asterisks of color
eclipse the blurred street names, transform the landscape.
In books, I find names worthy of a poet.
I ask my surgeon the proper term for my singular pair
of cataracts. He kindly spares me *senile*
although I'm 83 and the shoe fits.
Must I dissemble, sweeten
the pill with euphemism, and say I suffer from

senior cataracts? *Nuclear cortical,* my doctor says,
sending me off to global war and regions
of the brain that make me nervous. I toy with metaphoric
names that please the mind's
eye and tame my disorder: *Snowflake… Snowstorm,* I try.
Then *Sunflower…* Perhaps *Glassblower's
Cataract.* I substitute *Cuneiform*
from Persia: ancient rock inscriptions. Or those of
Babylon on brick and stone, a secret

code, made-to-order
for Scorpios, *Cuneiform;* white opaque, wedgelike,
sometimes called *Arrowhead,* ranged in
spokes around the cortex border. One left: *Spindle*
to get a handle on the matter. Starlight
again in my eyes because Spindle's tied to those
of us who spin—that eight-legged
spider whose spinnerets veil my eye and bar
light from the lens.

Simple Questions

My friend, the priest, you kept a simple pine box
on end in your living room.
It served as a conversation piece, good for
a couple of shocks when a guest
watched you take out the towels reserved
for an overnight visit.

We gave you our full attention, took care
not to ask, *What is it?* Imagined the box
lined with white satin, a whiter
face on the pillow, rosary twined around the cold
hand, and a spray of yellow roses on the black
drape at the foot.

                    When you disappeared south of
the Rio Grande, did you rush like the whiskey priest
in Graham Greene from the far-reaching
arms of the law into the arms of your lover?
And where is the pine box now? Have the towels
worn thin with waiting

                      for the uninvited guest,
the uncollected bones of the priest,
and the dark earth's kiss of greeting?

Dressing the Dead Girl by Gustave Courbet

Under the portrait of the bride, the nude figure
of the dead girl. When the auctioneer
lets the gavel fall, she has already crossed over,
but greed for gold has revived her. Imagine
the forger lifting her limp left arm,
closing her fingers on

                a mirror. Retitled *Dressing*
the Bride, the canvas replicates contradiction.
A handmaiden washes the girl's feet
like a Magdalen. To the right, four women intent
on their prayer books, the white
of their dresses almost

                lifting them out of shadow.
Behind them, a group of vague others, each with
a task to perform. One places a teapot
on a table. Two women on the left
spread a tablecloth or make up
the marriage bed. Why

                should the odor of death
suffuse this room whose colors are
those of mourning? Can it be that the maid's true
lover is the Robber Bridegroom
who lives in the heart's deep forest? And why
does the ghostly face

                in the mirror, the man's
looking over her shoulder, look like

someone we know? This must be the phantom
at the bottom of the well.
Iron fist in a velvet glove, driving the world
since the world began.

An Elegy for Dan

*For the faces of sorrow, I need only look within, open the
Book of Grief, where all of us have our stories.*

JOSEPH STROUD

Five months wearing your face in my heart's locket
and still, the image I trace
springs alive at my touch. You are always at work
creating your art. Now I watch you
transform the narrow room of your coffin
as you do every space you call
Home. Carpentry skills

                are a given. When you cut
rectangles in the low ceiling, roof windows
welcome renegade sun. Light floods the transparent
panel with color, casket become
cathedral. An accident shattered your fictional
covers for *Life* but granted you brief
reprieve. You are

             everywhere in these rooms
where you leave me reliquary treasures: brass lamp
inset with stained glass; woodprint of
Martin Luther King; cloth sculpture of a dying
Christ from your thesis show. Your talent
is a torrent renewing parched earth.

Standing before your portrait, clipped from a
magazine, framed to hang on my wall, I see you
for once in your clericals: Roman
collar, black suit, half-smile glinting off your

black-rimmed glasses. Behind you, something I call
a rose window haloes your head.
In my Book of Grief, I turn to a favorite page:

You in the driver's seat of my 1970 Nova, and me
beside you. Together, we're
heading west into our true country.

The Visionary under the Knife

Unstable as an overturned beetle—left eye prepped
and draped—I lie on the operating
table. On this final day of the year, the surgeon
will remove the identical twin preachers in the one
pulpit by the papal flag and the distant
fire hydrant down the block
that looks like a vicious green dog. The crew

waits for the Nurse with the Knives. Of course
I wear an IV in my arm, tape across
my brow and ankles, terror in my solar plexus.
Team members talk to one another
in low Medicalese: *capsulorrhexis… paracentesis
tract… phacoemulsification.* The oximeter
clipped to my middle finger

                              must be keeping time
with my pulse. Something else: a speculum locks my
eyelids open. If I could clearly see
what everyone else is doing, I would not be
here. Masked faces draw closer. These costumes
suggest a royal ball, a bank heist, a Halloween
party. I dramatize

                    all three. The glass eye of
the operating microscope zooms in
on the surgical field. Dr. Chen makes a stab
incision at the five o'clock
position, perhaps to revise ad slogans, mangled
by weak eyes, on my small TV.
Anesthetic drops allow the doctor to dissolve

the lens in quarters. That's when I issue orders:
Leave the eyelid movies untouched!
They are my favorite show to watch as I'm
drifting into dream. The room fills with jets of
spraying water and ultrasound far beyond
the human ear as the hollow needle vibrates 40,000
times a second. The needle stops. The doctor

inserts a foldable silicone lens, courtesy of
Bausch & Lomb. The surgeon
checks the wound for leaks. More anesthetic drops.
Tomorrow is a new year. Circus colors of falling
stars. Dazzle of meteors from oncoming
cars fades to Seattle gray. Metal patch over gauze
dressing attached

            to my operated eye. My trusty
gurney-on-standby carries me to Recovery,
body propped high enough to sip my java
and order tardy breakfast.
Time to leave but not the way I came. Doors
swing open on the ever-moving world
always and never the same.

Two

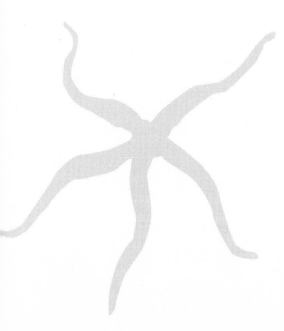

The Poetry of Spiders

Who knows if they sing in their webs? McPherson asks.
Unlike Little Miss Muffet, who bolted
in fright, she links spiders to music in spite of
Frost's design. *A dimpled spider, fat and white,*
sounds cute enough until we spot the *moth… dead wings
carried like a paper kite.* In Gallagher's poem,
beginning to say No *is to wear a tarantula in your*

buttonhole / yet smile invitingly. Most spiders don't
devour their mates, we tell ourselves,
and screw our courage to the sticking point, less
confident when we confront the Black Widow
whose red hourglass calls up Lowell's *spiders…
Swimming from tree to tree that mildewed day… Where
gnarled November makes* them *fly.*

                    If we could learn to
harvest spider silk, we'd breed mini-machines for
silk production and bleed Whitman's
noiseless patient spider. But that's been tried and
failed. A better way to go: join Wrigley's
walk along the forest path and read the signs: *tatters
of… webs, wind-swung, / making of his dark shirt and jeans*

an odd diaphanous tweed. Spiders hide in layers of myth
as complicated as their webs: Arachne's suicide,
Meleager's murder. In his story, we learn
that amber comes from birds' tears. Should McPherson be
onto something, who knows if a spider,
trapped in fossil resin, may sing from that ornamental
prison to create a bird-and-spider duet?

Mythology of Spider Silk

Skein upon skein of thread in rainbow colors—
silk of silver and gold as well—
heaped beside the peasant girl whose claim to rival
Athena's skill as a weaver will soon
be tested. Beside each loom, the raw stuff
that will prove who is the better
at her craft.

       The signal given, shuttles fly. Athena's
fabric, as expected, dazzles the eye.
Arachne's, finished at the same moment, no less
impressive. The goddess, in a jealous
fury, slits Arachne's web
from top to bottom, then beats the maiden
about the head with a shuttle.

       Disgraced and angry,
Arachne hangs herself. At that, a slight regret
steals into Athena's heart. She
lifts the body from the noose, sprinkles the corpse
with magic liquid. As if from sleep,
Arachne stirs, comes back to life as a spider, her
skill at spinning, preserved.

Three Things That Make Me Outrageously Happy in March

Begin with the evergreen *Clematis montana.* Shy
about opening, blooms pulse into view
a few at a time against the night sky. Some
morning, a creamy tsunami
sweeps over the chain-link fence in a spring
seizure of yearning. Drenches the passerby in
dizzying scent and charges winter's
dark air without warning.

                     Next, the black umbrella
ribs of *Styrax japonica* open to rain. Their
delicate green incipient leaves
reverse the gradual losses of autumn. Remember
this overture to the Japanese Snowbell
symphony in May when it's time to clean up
the carpet of dried flowers and pods, time to
cart uprooted seedlings away.

                     When navel oranges,
kissed by lazy California sun, glow like
moons in every supermarket, I go
crazy, buy all I can carry. At home, they
tumble from the sack to kiss my eager lips, and as
that nectar of the gods floods my veins, I live
in lovers' paradise every juicy moment
of Seattle rains.

Spiders in Camouflage

On damp moss and leaf litter, the small spider
conserves water she needs to stay
alive. In the war against water loss, she
wears thick armor. Knows how to spin a tiny
orb-web. The size of a pinhead
is her measure; home, a hiding place
among debris

           on the soil surface. Fortunately,
the tricks of this spider are as good as
Houdini's: to mimic inanimate objects—flowers
and dead leaves. To imitate ants, those insects
famous for their painful bite.
To intimidate predators, a spider
walks zigzag, waving

           the front pair of legs like
antennae. The Jumping Spider from Borneo
copies a species of wasp without a wing. This
back-to-front posture
disguises the hindmost quarter as the head of
her model, abdomen raised,
fangs prepared for the sting.

Synthesizing Spider Silk

Dragline silk: the fiber from which spiders make
the scaffold for their webs. These threads
have been found in the stratosphere, seven miles
above the sea. Reported by a sharp-eyed
sky traveler, who spotted the filigree
floating in still air. In two world wars, these
sundew webs were considered chemical warfare.
Darwin, too, had noted

           that a Gossamer Spider
coated the rigging of his ship, the *Beagle*, several
times as it lay in harbor
in the Río de la Plata. Imagine the unlikely regatta
in which the best sailboat
loses the race, thanks to that inveterate
spinner. Clouds were once thought to be built of
similar material. Pliny speaks of the year
it rained wool. Maybe *web and pin,*
an old name for cataract,

           came from pulling the wool
over one's eyes. The three Fates may have been
the original weavers. The first
spun the thread of life. The second
assigned man his destiny. The third, most feared,
carried the horrid shears that cut off the thread
forever. Twice as elastic as nylon,
draglines today are bioengineered. Waterproof,
stretchable, five times

stronger than steel, they
are still weaker than the real silk
produced by the web-spinning spider.

Lodestar

That spring when hawthorns flushed rose to red
along Archery Row and, on campus,
the rolling lawn spread green as receding tides
under everyday Oregon rain, I knelt
in the convent chapel
trying to pray, my head a hive
where distractions

                buzzed in and out, each
with a load of nectar. The Sisters had
already vacuumed, dusted, polished the sanctuary.
Had unrolled the starched white
linens and evened the ends just so. I could tell
by the clink of glass and the sound of
running water, they were

                making bouquets for
the altar. At last the young novice emerges
bearing a vase of roses nearly as tall
as she is, shifts the arrangement twice, and
kneels on the altar step
for a moment of adoration. I wait for her to
get up, bring in

                the matching bouquet, but she
remains anchored in place like the *Queen Mary*,
radiance flooding her bows, her body
seeming to levitate like a ship riding the waves.
What sweetness distilled in the honeycomb
leaves so little room for a gaze like hers
locked on the Heart of Light?

Electrical Impulses

for Lia Purpura

It's August and we're cooling off in camp chairs
on the back deck where it's half dark. You raise
your arms to lift the long hair
from your neck when the motion-detector lights
flash on. What a power surge for a poet! You
wait for the bulbs to go black
then fling your arms

                    again—*two wild arms in the air*
waving – as they finally did to scare off the bee—
now bent on illumination. How we wish that
this magical trick would work when we sit down to
write. You repeat the gesture two or
three times, invoking a modern muse, not Electra,
the Lost Pleiad, who

                    withdrew from the star cluster
and appears in the sky only now and then,
but her distant descendant. Watching your childlike
delight, I'm thinking you're in the electric
chair, current on high, not making your heart quit
but blasting it wide open. Not
dimming your imagination, your

                     vision, but exciting
them as amber—the Greeks' *elektron* – is excited by
friction and becomes, as the *OED*
has it, "notably *electric.*" You're right: we share

So, what do you think?

Book Title: _____

Comments: _____

_____

_____

_____

Can we quote you on that? ☐ yes ☐ no

Copper Canyon Press seeks to build the awareness of, appreciation of, and audience for a wide range of emerging and established American poets, as well as poetry in translation from many of the world's cultures, classical and contemporary. To receive our catalog, send us this postage-paid card or email your contact information to poetry@coppercanyonpress.org

NAME: _____

ADDRESS: _____

CITY: _____

STATE: _____ ZIP: _____

EMAIL: _____

☐ Send me *Editor's Choice*, a bimonthly email of poems from forthcoming titles.

COPPER CANYON PRESS

www.coppercanyonpress.org

BUSINESS REPLY MAIL

FIRST-CLASS MAIL   PERMIT NO. 43   PORT TOWNSEND WA

POSTAGE WILL BE PAID BY ADDRESSEE

Copper Canyon Press
PO Box 271
Port Townsend, WA 98368-9931

a dangerous art. We'd feel thankful
to be notably electric. Tonight is a start. We
happily make the most of it.

The Magdalen with the Nightlight
by Georges de La Tour

The candle plumbs a sadness in her gaze
that stems the flood of memories each night
when spirit mounts a watch the blood betrays.

Body resumes the phosphorescent haze,
its diagram of burning appetite.
The candle plumbs a sadness in her gaze.

The holy books, the skull, the peace she prays
for: all enemies of passionate delight.
Her spirit mounts. A watch the blood betrays

transforms the glittering evil into grays.
She undergoes again the soul's Dark Night
as candles plumb a sadness in her gaze.

Light and reflected light are no surprise.
The painter knows art's power to translate
when spirit mounts a watch the blood betrays.

Her past is quick to challenge, calmly lays
a bet that seven devils will requite
the flame a candle plumbs in her sad gaze.
The spirit mounts a watch. The blood betrays.

On My Sixtieth Birthday, I Work at the Yellow Sun

1979

Sunday. I am mopping up spills in the oils with the young.
On time as I begin my next iambic decade
making poems in the cooler of the universal co-op. Never won
an NEA, a Guggenheim, a handout from the American
Council of Learned Societies, the NEH, or the Rockefeller
fellers.

     In spite of villanelles beside the shallow bird
feeder, I consider the anapests, how they grow
among the ruminant Final Readers. Happy out of habit,
cutting the big cheeses, I ask myself how they
age so rich in rhyme, too highly seasoned for my taste,
when I must step carefully past the elbow
macaroni and real bristle brushes
merely to get by.

     We are all workers here. We do not
qualify for easy money, fenugreek and choriamb, cheap yogurt,
the perennial sestina. I weave through dead legumes: split
pea and lentil, the beans—soy, kidney, lima. Steep
yogi tea in my head amid the crush of tarragon and cloves,
coriander, cardamom, lemon verbena. My jeans
flourish among the sprouts and peanuts, the whole
grains and dried fruits, the pure clover
honey of the Yellow Sun.

     Still it would be nice to win
a free ride on the mood elevator with the Yale
lock. To step inside the Critics Circle, charmed by

a second's look, board a surface train for Coquilles
St. Jacques and the Pulitzer, break the downhill
cycle of trochees and dactyls. ("Never make it big by
pedaling.") Next stop, the Nobel. Forget
the Lamont people. A Calimyrna fig to the fickle
trustees of inflated dollars for the PSA
in any form or freedom.

                    In my sixtieth November, let me
stay, not straining gnats beside the shrill
menstrual sponges, the colanders and paring knives,
regalia of the Bard-behind-the-Grille. Try
Khadrawi dates on a Little Magazine rather than
blush unseen. Milk the unpasteurized
editor for all he can give, haywagon pried from the stars.
Better late (and less) than inorganic

                              sour grapes. Let me
sprint to a lyrical finish out-of-print, a modest
royalty. Not given a riotous living, I'll take
twenty years more behind bars—sunlight and music—roses
and muses, prisoner of the Yellow Sun.

Spider Folklore

To counteract a fever, old wives favor a believer
who wears a spider in a nutshell
round his neck. When bile-yellow stains the skin,
the cure of choice for jaundice:
swallow a large house spider

                        rolled up in butter.
Arachnids on lapel or sleeve are said to be a sign
of luck—money wrapped in silk. I've always
washed these shy intruders
down the drain or swatted them to spider-heaven,
but as a poet, I prefer

                    creative fiction, bold
images, to sterile fact. The old wives guarantee
powers of invention, my physical
and fiscal health. Remember this when you
see cobwebs in my house.

Delicate Pleasures

Every morning I pick a fresh bouquet of sweet peas
and two stems of maidenhair fern. Put them in a small
royal blue vase under the spice cupboard
where sun will not fade them, and study their medley
of colors. They say the perfect
bouquet must always include some white. So I rush out
at 6 a.m. for the shades
overnight has delivered. More hues from the mixmaster:
after a series of

                  cardinal reds to burgundy, cameo pink,
orchid to plum and madder violet, suddenly white! I cut
the lone blossom at once so that others
will open. Today, checking the flowers' highwire act
next to the garden gate, I see that tendrils
intended for climbing have a stranglehold on a vivid
red beauty and will not let go. I sever fine ties,
lift the wry-necked corolla from its
captors, whose murder

                  recalls my favorite whodunit,
The Oxford Companion to the Mind. In its pages,
I find a factor in color perception
called *spectral waves.* Does color vanish when there's
no eye to devour it? I wave to the specter
of my garden, ghostly in afternoon haze. That high
wolf-whistle can't come from a cardinal,
must be a mimic—starling, perhaps—of the mynah
family, well known for chatter.

Called *grackle* in
India. Audubon credits this darling with seductive
calls. I admit he does turn my head. Daybreak:
sweet rain falls on the cheek of berry
and bloom after days of drought. Raspberries
double in size. In the language
of flowers, Sweet Pea stands for Delicate Pleasures,
doomed to capsize in their
ultimate meaning: Departure.

Three

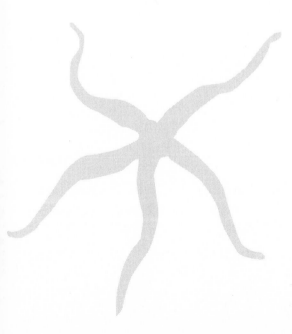

The poetry of earth

               is never dead, as John Keats
testified before they lowered him to earth.
At 25, racked lungs deprived of air, he died
in Rome—1821—a world away from
Fanny Brawne, his stone nameless as he wished.
Already the great odes stood,
his testament:

             To Autumn, On a Grecian Urn, and
To a Nightingale. If Conrad Aiken's
Stars… Pale in a saffron mist and seem to die,
they only *seem* because the eye
retains the afterglow as if the stars
were flowers—Roethke's *Cut stems struggling
to put down feet,*

           a resurrection Bishop
understands: the iceberg *cuts its facets from within.*
Like jewelry from a grave. At Keats's tomb
his lines echo and reecho, alive and
resonant as voices from a cave. *All through the dark*
Merwin's night wind *looks*
for the grief it belongs to.

            On precious stone, not
far from the Tiber, Keats ordered this
inscription—for his brief life, the perfect
metaphor—*Here lies One Whose Name was writ in Water.*
Now water carries it to the farthest shore.

Questions of Interior Decoration

Expert in their craft, although uninvited, spiders
sign on to decorate my home. They
belong to the Weavers Industrial Union, can give
their friends a leg up and still have
seven to spare. They weave

                    silk curtains on window
ledges, suspend gray swatches from the chandelier.
Sun conspires with their artistry
to show the observant gold filigree they call to
my lax attention. Draglines

                    brush my trespasser
face and skeins attached to the picture frames
cling to the hand that removes them. I
regret the uneasy moment I wear a small, white
spider in my near-white hair. Why

                    is it these
ornaments remain invisible until I sit down with
a guest whose wandering eye
rolls over my living room—ceiling to wall to
window—highlighting how laggardly
I gear myself up to housekeep?

Two for Wallace Stevens

I. FLORAL STUDY

Description is revelation.
WALLACE STEVENS

The lazy clay Susan holds the stoneware pitcher
holding the flowers, blends opaque gray
with lavender shadows, darker
flecks, and the faraway thumbprints of the potter.
Brown lip and handle mimic the brown
stripes above and below the deep
blue base that keeps the pitcher grounded.

These modest hues yield the stage to a bricolage
of floral charges: an odd couple of
colors—coral Oriental poppies reminiscent
of the poet's *pine and coral and coraline sea* – and
rose peonies. Together, they draw me back
to a slight dissonance. I drink disharmony in
as if I've defeated the spectrum.

                              Poppies hoard
their broad petals, open wide indoors, seductive
as opium. Their sultry purple-black
stamens drowse at the center, with one jagged
scar to match on each
coral petal. No wonder they impeach the peony's
color, whose double pinks
close on themselves, prodigal with perfume.

When, one by one, poppies scatter at a touch, languid
as a stripper, purple dust
pollinates everything in sight. Narrow-toothed
peonies collapse in clusters, fall
to the turntable, layers of sweet disorder.
The exhausted ballerina steps out of her pastel
costume, petals in disarray around her
all the way to her knees.

Irrational moment its unreasoning... when the moon
hangs on the wall / Of heaven-haven.
WALLACE STEVENS

From Logic to Nightmare, one critic writes,
the poem mediates extremes of order
and disorder. This morning as I write, Chaos
surrounds me, the state that Wallace Stevens
thought to tame

          by framing it in Logic larger
than Reason. His "Connoisseur of Chaos"
flaunts a syllogistic flair
that charms the reader with false premises
beyond mere argument: a logic, as it were,
of feeling when

          the coastline stretches far
enough to capture pattern. He gives us *shade*
Of a cloud on sand, a shape
on the side of a hill: two proofs
of relation—hence,

          of order. He surprises
bulletins from the Muse chalked on sidewalks,
concludes with a floating eagle
and *the intricate Alps.* Tonight when I pass by
coral poppies and pink peonies
reconciled in a gray

          pitcher, I believe that
in that clay grip I will see

flowers of South Africa blooming *on the tables of*
Connecticut and be persuaded by
the poet's propositions.

                  The clash of colors
may reflect conflicting views that intersect in
poems, a harmony of opposites
not *posed,* as Stevens says, *like statuary…*
in the Louvre.

The Spider in *Brewer's Dictionary*

Opened, the book released a small
spider: pale, nearsighted,
anonymous. No doubt a scholar of
phrase and fable, who preferred
investigating the shadows. Under
the kitchen's public light, the spider
flinched in the sudden
fluorescence. The meaning I wrenched
from this brief encounter: *Sweetest
to die doing the work you love best.*

Vascular Diagnostics

All over TV, weather sharks hooked on a feeding frenzy:
gale winds off the coast. It's my eighty-fifth
birthday, and I celebrate with a trip to Vascular
Diagnostics for a Doppler flow study and
an ultrasound scan. Will the weather inside my head
match the weather outside or dare to
contradict the storm?

                        The technician dabs gel on my right
temple where calcium debris in the semicircular canal
makes me dizzy. She peers into my brain
while I navigate Venice, hear arterial blood go *Swish*,
swish, *swish* on its way to the skull.
She says the view is "a dream" for someone my age,
which means bone doesn't

                        get in her way. The machine
lets her ponder my skull for a full hour. Left temple
next, where the view is obscure. Vertebral
artery, carotid, eyelid vessels, seven centimeters in
at the back of the eye. The head scan
shows a normal flow. Circulation, efficient,
my vertigo exactly the problem

                        I had guessed from reading
the Merck: a frightening, harmless disorder with a hefty
name: Benign Paroxysmal, Positional
Vertigo. Lasts for weeks or months. Uncontrollable
eye movements. No evidence of tumor in
the MRI. No hint of stroke. Only this
rumor of blood pulsing,

a rhythm straight from the heart
translated to the right-brain ear in the language of
poems both ears understand.

Time Exposure

for Tom Aslin

Seven days into winter, the kitchen counter
sags under the weight
of Lemon Boy tomatoes, house-ripened, ranged
in rows, with, here and there, an
Early Girl, red complement,

                           companion. Outdoors
later than ever putting my garden to bed.
Chickweed taking over
wherever I dig and stubborn seeds of volunteer
cherry tomatoes, last to die, plotting
to sabotage rivals

                I plant in the spring. Here
dogwood overlooks the skeletal
wisteria twined around the deck rail. I rake up
the rain of magnolia leaves from my neighbor's
tree and prune the raspberry canes

                       as they
take on the pale green cast of envy. Envoy
extraordinaire of photosynthesis
at work, fat buds of clematis prepare for a March
opening. They pull me back indoors to stand
in the south window, the mind's eye

                         fixed on bloom.
Each creamy sepal stipples the fence and drenches
evergreen leaves in fragrance.

I remember your charge—*Memorize them for me*—and
send this verbal image, urging
the season forward until the darkroom
in the brain resolves this faded winter light.

Confidence Man

Your brain a cache for every American Dream—money,
love, fame—success most of all—you
wanted your name on a major public structure—one
you had built. You call to tell me you are
back on the Black Sea, homeless
at 29 in your home country, your airline ticket
courtesy of the cops.

                    The women you loved
loved money. One lied, sued, and lost. One loaded
your credit cards with debt
and slept with your brother. You don't know
what happened to your tools, the same tools I
ransomed from a crooked mover's extortion
scheme. You *don't know*

                    nothing. Except, of course,
that your country is really stupid and you
live alone on the streets. I know that I miss you,
look at your name on thousands in IOUs past due
in my files. In my will, I
forgive you the lot. On the phone, without being
asked, I say, *I can't give you*

                    another penny. That's
not the reason you called. You ask, *Are you okay?*
Request my prayers. Are you panhandling now when three
years ago you made 100 grand?
You said then, *Whatever do I want, I get it.* Like
the four-hundred-dollar brown
leather jacket you wore.

Your greatest fear was of
being deported. When the money lords
swooped down, claiming their pound of flesh, it was
just a matter of time till they
sold the clothes off your back. A last-ditch
confrontation followed by a month of silence
when your machine hung up
and I couldn't reach you.

On Christmas Day
you called and came over. I remember both of us
cried. Now that you're gone,
who will change the motion-sensor lights on my
deck? Replace the fluorescent tubes in the kitchen,
program the front-porch light?
I avoid the eyes in unshaven faces of men. Mute
stare and lank hair

of the women. I know the ghost
of your gaze would pierce my heart
where it floats on its own Black Sea, as if mourning
a son, unwilling still
to believe that I cannot trust you.

The Repentant Magdalen by Georges de La Tour

The candle limns a halo meant to stay
although the red dress hints a scarlet past.
Sinner and saint trade places every day.

What leads to this conversion, who can say?
A death's-head mounted on the ferry mast?
The candle limns a halo meant to stay.

One theme becomes a de La Tour cliché,
each painting simplified beyond the last.
Sinner and saint trade places every day

they walk along a brightly lit, broad way.
And bronze or bone, the skull's a grim forecast
the candle limns. A halo meant to stay

the siren song reverses to betray
digressions into regions of unrest
as sinner and saint trade places. Every day

bold art transforms the subtle interplay
of light and dark: circles more vast
than haloes candle-limned and meant to stay.
Sinner and saint trade places every day.

Serpentine Soliloquy

Start with the snake-in-the-Paradisal-grass,
the viper who tempted Eve in the garden.
Thence, to the sea serpent, Laocoön's curse
and that of his sons. They feared Greeks bearing gifts,
spoke out against the wooden horse.
In any case, the snake's best gift is poison.

One strand of Medusa's snaky locks would poison
everything around her—earth, sky, grass.
Give me that power. This comes straight from the horse's
mouth: Believe me when I say the ordinary garden
snake is harmless, but have you the gift
of herpetology? Without it, a curse

may fall on you and yours—curse
like the one that brought Cleopatra down: poison
asp held to her breast. That cobra's gift
to her was venomous death. *All flesh is grass*,
the Psalmist says, whether Death strike in the garden
or arrive in the bridal chamber. Suicide is a horse

of another color. The one who saddles that horse
may learn the true ancestral curse,
his will surprised in the pleasant haze of the garden
by reptiles bent on injecting poison.
Remember the narrow Fellow in the Grass
and Emily's Zero at the Bone? A gift

unlike any other, but look that gift
horse in the mouth. The winged horse

of poetry may graze too long on the grass
skirt of your private life, a curse
that threatens to make the gift of art poison
that withers fruit and flower in the garden.

Hallucinatory snakes may haunt the garden
unfortunate poets walk, belated gift
from years of downing alcoholic poison.
The sober infant Hercules rode a dark horse
till found in his crib, attacked by Hera's curse.
Two great snakes, limp as withered grass,

clenched like garden tools or reins of a horse
in either hand: gift from Hera, a curse
on Zeus whose poison seed flourishes still like grass.

After a tearful morning

                        I take myself to the backyard
to drown my woes in a pool of sweat, a cure
as old as Eden. Hours undoing
the work of sun and rain in my garden: 8-inch grasses
choking out tomatoes. Miles of
wild mustard running amok in the winter squash.
Slugs   earwigs   snails

                    making a lacework of lettuce.
I drag the beanstalk ladder from the general
clutter in my garage to bring down
Blue Lake beans, stretching like Jack to retrieve them.
I count on their magic to help me
steal a bag of gold from the ogre. When that wide
white road unspools before me,

                        I follow it to a
threshold. Here in the heart of danger, risking my
life in the oven, I count on
the ogre's wife to weave a pattern of lies
to sustain me. After a dull interlude when words
desert me, I manage to steal
the ogre's hen and the single

                        word that summons her
golden eggs. Not content with one theft, I steal
his magic harp as well, command it
to sing away sadness, trusting the spell of music,
rescue of words returned
in the pale green light I have
opened my eyes to for decades.

Four

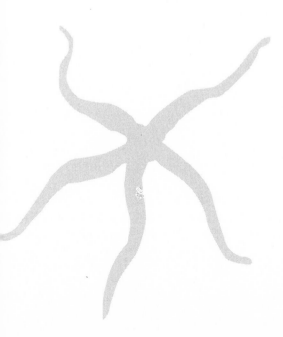

The Poetry of Swans

October twilit water under the wild swans at Coole
Mirrors a still sky. Against all evidence
a former world believed
swans sing their sweetest when about to die
and, on that premise, called its greatest poets
swans: Homer, Swan of Maeander,
Virgil, of Mantua, and Shakespeare, Swan of Avon.

Merrill's Black Swan *has learned to enter / Sorrow's
lost secret center,* and the Black Swan
Jarrell encounters on the lake after milking
opens a *red beak: inside… darkness… stars and
the moon.* The waterbirds settle down
on a pond with reeds and sedge, each to ponder
its own image

               in the black reflective waters where
the rushes grow. *No swan… so fine* as Marianne's
*chintz china one with… toothed gold / collar on
to show whose bird it was.* In the mind's
eye, the watcher sees a mixed flotilla of legendary
swans glide shoreward over silver
waves to animate the shallows, while far away

on still St. Mary's Lake, Wordsworth's solitary swan
Floats double, swan and shadow. A shot rings out.
From a height, one whistling swan
falls, crippled, to the water. His departure
song—melodious, soft-muted—a better way to die,
uniting myth and truth in a vain
struggle to rejoin companions in the sky.

Astronomy

This bird-woman flew to my kitchen wall, high
above the sink—a bibelot made of
coconut shell from Mexico—woman I call
my Aztec Sun. Sun-yellow
frames her painted cheeks, and six
symmetrical rays surround them, each: red
yellow, and green.

                    Eyebrows fallen parentheses,
lips a small star, it's clear that she's
missing her starfish brother. Fossils show: 300
million years before dinosaurs, Blood Star
plunged to the ocean floor.
Aztec remembers. Replays the scene
evenings when sun sets red in the west.

The Courtship of Birds

The Arena Bird, known also as the Sage Grouse,
struts in the dancing-ground,
inflates the yellow air sacs on his breast
and spreads the long pointed feathers of his tail.
His only role, to make himself
available to females. But first, he must be
noticed: he booms and toots and coos,

promotes his suit with sound effects. This lover
breeds but does not brood.
Nest-building time, and the Grouse is out of there!
Consider that Eurasian Sandpiper
who wears, in breeding season, owl-like ear
tufts and his Elizabethan collar—stiff,
encircling—from which

                        he earns his name, the Ruff.
From such exotic sources comes the stuff of
nuns' habits. Witness the Sisters of the Holy Cross
who valued something like the ruff
to frame their faces: a tube of starched white
cloth, crimped on a stick
and baked in the oven. Nothing's

                   too good for
a bride of the Lord. The Peacock spreads his train,
vibrates the quills with rustling
sound, turns from side to side before his mate,
a model in a fashion show. The Barn-door Cock,
with drooping wing, circles close
around his hen who waits for him to mount.

The Bowerbird constructs a mating place, decorates
the house to impress the female. She will
choose the rendezvous whose decor suits her fancy.
If drabber males build complicated
hideouts, the flashier set, tricked out in black
and orange, in glimmering gold,
erect more modest arbors. The female enters her

boudoir where the builder takes her on tour, tail
cocked high, bill pointing to his "painting,"
walls stained with a tool gripped in
his beak and dipped in natural pigment. His treasure
cache includes plastic, berries, bone, fruit,
tinfoil, blue feathers: he's a savvy designer.
He mates with many females, philanderer,
not a provider. His women

                    fly off to build nests
and raise their young apart. Only birds,
of all the animals, grow feathers. Whether a bird
drums on dead limbs like a woodpecker or
booms in spring marshes with the bittern, mating
is always the female's choice. For every
feather in his cap, an enemy slain—perhaps by an
arrow through the lover's heart.

To a Former Lover in His Sanctuary

Here in this lyrical retreat you planned and
coined a name for, the play of light
I cannot see, except through the camera's
less-than-candid lens, goes on
without me. From the wicker wing chair, you
glance away from the *Journal of Aesthetics*
in a timed reprieve

                    from philosophic thought.
Against all reason, why do I grieve, who
ought to rejoice in your solitude? Why does
the snapshot make me feel
like a widow, half-life banished without
a trace? In a charmed circle, clay
birds cruise a symphony

                    of blues. Blue waves
crawl the architectural shore. Clandestine
clues flutter, commonplace as a stilled
word, withheld caress. Italian mosaics cling
to the brick wall, echo the floor
tiles. Anything more, spare as an extra
jigsaw piece.

                    Dinner guests the night we met, we
built your new terrazza, phrase by
phrase. Discussed the enemy weather, the skills
required. Faithful as a Muse, I
sent you Greek mosaic postcards every day
that week. Now the chair that matches yours
stands idle.

The credible pelican's absurd bill
remains forever closed. And I must
give these two-dimensional figures, flat and pale,
body and metaphoric life, however brief,
until the hard mosaic elements can be composed.

The scissor-tailed swallow

                              dives from the cliff
and the pale air is altered if only
a little. Reversing figure and ground
the eye reads negative shapes,
a Matisse cutout. When the shaken air
releases its hold we know
that the true art is living. "Was it a *real* bird?"
someone asks: steel-blue-

                      black in the unlucky
light facing a cold April. Already another
I inserts the quicksilver body
into a cliffside hole   the cardboard
well of the puzzle. Wingshadow deepens
river and stone   clouds the remembered face
of the canyon. Flight

                        inscribed on the air's
blank page   lingers awhile   a skywritten
passage   characters drifting to various shapes
like lines of a poem   the reader
walks through by radar. If, as Freud thought,
writing begins as the voice
of the absent   a way across the ravine   the word

may go on without us   uncertain and sure   gold
as the sunset curtain   flung back
against the vault   by the hand's trajectory
bold as a falcon.

Paula Executes the Angels

By rights this should have been an easy piece,
if art is ever easy. Paula, the sculptor-nun,
the angels, and the woman from the church
committee who brought the two together.
The first sketch shows three horizontal figures
with flowing robes and trumpets flaring out

like necks of Canada geese. Tossed out
because, the woman says, she's made a piece
of fiction. Angels with feet? False figures!
The next, she finds too thin, too young, and none
quite masculine enough, but altogether
foolish. That ponytail, for instance. Church

elders would never approve. To please the church
she'll have to round the scrawny figures out,
feather their wings, and pull herself together
to meet the next demand. No hope for peace
and a free hand or the calm life every nun
aspires to as she contemplates the figures

of windowed saints whose steady gaze prefigures
heaven. But this is still an earthly church,
so back to work! The challenge for this nun:
to find some middle ground and tough it out,
not merely to create an altarpiece
but to release both art and prayer together.

When Paula tries again, she ties together
the woman's charge and purely spirit figures

who stand on principle, not feet, their peace
a tribute to the universal church:
waistlines and thighs, a trifle plump and out-
wardly almost defiant as if none

were not gaining slowly on the sculptor-nun.
When next the middlewoman gets together
with the artist, they work the contract out
and rubber-stamp the art-commissioned figures
surrendered to the keeping of the church
that, in a way, is father to the piece.

This feisty nun, that woman good at figures
appear together—one—before the client church,
each having worked out her uneasy piece.

To a Crow Outside My Bay Window

When have I ever welcomed you to my gutters,
stuck on the one wrong note
Poe's Raven returned forevermore? Litany and
response, my every invocation
draws down the repeated guttural cry
your mate doubles from a telephone wire
high overhead.

          When I stomp my foot, clap
my hands, rattle venetian blinds, you flap away,
but there's no mistake: you're
on a round-trip with no plans to brake anywhere
but over my eaves, morning and noon
all summer. Am I expected to ask you in,
terrific newcomer mimic?

              You do have a language
mostly scold, a memory better than mine
for bold aggression. Smartest of birds, your
fossils revealed in deposits 12 million years
old in Colorado, what chance do I have
with an omen? Go back to your nest! My
nuisance, Nemesis, shadow at my window.

After great pain, a formal feeling comes

It wasn't formal exactly. More like a hummingbird
in the midst of a crow convention: black
cries so raucous they seemed a mockery of common
speech. And the hummer's ultrasonic
whir: wings going nowhere

                    over the hearts of flowers,
hovering. What's more, the pain may have been
less than great because it was mainly
physical, the lot of one not ruby-throated but
undeniably in the pink.

              Now I cast my fate with
that of the world's smallest bird, impaled on a
purple thistle. With peril every way I turn, and
prone to accident, I earn my
badge of courage diving at eagles, those colossal

birds of prey, deadly as picture windows. Along
the way, my song is mouselike
squeaks, the drone of wings in flight. My heart,
like the heart of the hummingbird,
equals 20 percent of my weight.

                  Day after wrenching
day, I contemplate death, linger over Baltimore
orioles, big frogs, tropical
spiders whose insects feed my hunger. The spider
silk I wrap around my nest, I ornament with lichen.

Windswept into the river, the current taking over,
I could drown. But I have work to do,
must join the hummingbird to go the distance. Among
the large diurnal fowl—hawks, vultures,
and kites—flight patterns are silhouettes soaring

overhead. Canada geese migrate in formal Vs. Like
the hummer, I fill my small crop
with nectar and hope to take my leave mining
the deepest cup in the floral kingdom: red
throat of the trumpet creeper.

The Wild Parrots

Spring. And our neighborhood waits the return of
parakeets, escaped from a pet owner's
cage to fend for themselves in Seattle yards.
Half screech, these birds vie with the crow
as they settle on weeping
willow and birch. In Flannery's Church of Christ
without Christ, a palpable

                          absence makes itself
felt. Where are the birds this year?
Gone with the glitter of Christmas baubles
dazzled by sun on sheen? Tired of being a know-it-all
I borrow a leaf from the parakeet.
Study the aerodynamics of flight, earn a degree in
Parakeet as a Second Language.

                          Remembered, the birds
are real, travel in screaming and squawking
flocks, unravel the gift of tongues. *I go to prepare
a place.* Canary-yellow, their wings
stitch earth and sky together. When a bird
falls to the ground, your Heavenly Father knows.
Your worth is more than that of
many sparrows. Not doves

                          this week, but fiery
tongues along the avenue where we huddle in fear
and wait. The moment we feel most
forsaken, we hear the beat of birdwings. Recognize

the envoys known to strengthen and
console. Our caged hearts open to
the Wild Paraclete.

Five

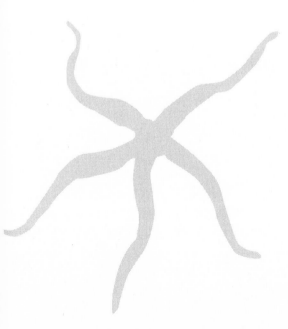

A Crown of Sonnets for "The King"

I. THE UNDERTAKER'S DREAM

Around the Oklahoma copper casket,
the dream stars Army buddies playing taps,
heartbreak hotel the sum of all your trips
while thousands stand in line to buy a ticket.
Elvis, it's hard to screw your swiveling hips
tight as a lightbulb into this final socket,
your body carried away in the gold lamé jacket
as something keeps breaking loose and the music stops.

When Charlie Hodge, with deft mascara brush,
tenderly changed to black your temples' gray
the "Memphis Mafia" knew how to make
the most of loyalty amid the crush.
Stand back and let him breathe. Don't go away!
These are the words I hear as I awake.

These are the words I hear as I awake
to strangers at the gate and cameras in the trees,
to stunned and stunning women, Lisa Marie's
They say my daddy's dead. Will he come back?
The helter-skelter, harum-scarum, hurly-burly blues
settle on Graceland with unwelcome news,
the sad world quaking in the aftershock.

It takes the strongest five to lift "The King"
onto a stretcher, past the spiral stares,
his aides forming a wall, a sturdy shield.
Hardheaded woman in tears, Ginger can't do anything
so Vernon takes her in the house to join his prayers
although the mourners know his fate is sealed.

3. DOA

Although the mourners know his fate is sealed
they can't give up on God, Who may come through.
They cast about for something more to do:
into Emergency, the patient's wheeled.
The human curtain parts. Aides leave the field
to doctors who inject the heart and who
start IV drips, then shock a time or two
the organ grown so large with caring that it failed.

Why are we working on this corpse? The nurse
throws up her hands. The crew, shocked back to normal,
admits discretion is the better part of valor.
They'll stare suspicion down, advise, rehearse
the clothes that Elvis wears for his last formal.
Up to this moment, blue was his favorite color.

Up to this moment, blue was his favorite color:
sky blue and baby blue and aquamarine.
But not this rigor mortis blue. He'd draw the line,
be all shook up remembering the squalor
that welcomed him to Tupelo, his frailer
twin stillborn. In poverty we end, as we begin:
the helpless welfare father in the shotgun
shack, the mother's pierced heart like the Virgin's dolor.

And there are voices when the music blurs.
They charge into the room, however sterile,
bounce off the wall, the ceiling, and the bed:
voices of snooty critics and the jealous stars,
the mother's baby talk, the lover's quarrel,
Sinatra's taking back the words he said.

Sinatra's taking back the words he said:
from Vegas to the Houston Astrodome,
the stars come out to light the sergeant home,
and Frankie's carpet, like his face, turns red.
He sends his daughter, Nancy, in his stead
with gifts for Elvis, her smile like polished chrome,
presenting lacy dress shirts for the optimum
impact on this returning demigod.

The jailhouse rock performer switches roles
to tux and dress blues from a biker's leather.
He's learned a thing or two about romance
which sends his movies higher in the polls.
His costars know he has his act together:
they walk the glittering runway in a trance.

6. PARADE OF BEAUTIFUL WOMEN

They walk the glittering runway in a trance,
this Odyssean gathering of shades:
women in silk and satin, fine brocades,
all of them linked to Elvis, now advance:
Ann-Margret, Natalie Wood, Gail Ganley's dance,
Priscilla in her teens; the random raids
on Frank Sinatra's girlfriend, and the aides
recruiting women for the one-night stands.

Here's Tuesday, Kathy, Ginger, Joanna, June.
Here's Dottie Harmony, Anne Helm, Anita Wood
and any-way-you-want-me Dixie, Debra, Joyce.
Add Barbara Leigh and don't pass over Joan.
Elisabeth and all the rivals she withstood
while waiting in the shadows for his voice.

Still waiting in the shadows for your voice
a quarter-century later, year by year,
the faithful come to visit. They know that here
their hearts will find some comfort. Solace
attends their grieving, for this hallowed place
holds all you loved, creates an atmosphere
familiar as the songs that keep you near
and so alive that thousands make the choice.

It's tranquil here and you're asleep at last,
your numbers and your parents' carved in stone.
Some fan who wept with you left roses in a basket.
No need of pills for sleep. That day is past.
Friends gather, so you'll never sleep alone,
around the Oklahoma copper casket.

Figures for a Carrousel

I. THE MAN

If someone took away the shield his last attack
would be the bull-like head
and that splayed word he angles toward the sky.
Pain ripples out along the ribs,
draws the navel in. Stumps of old wounds
tell what limbs he shed to win this bronze
reprieve, protection from above.

Leonardo said a painter could find a battle scene
in lichen marks on a wall. The pebble
Henry Moore picked up contained this warrior's
leg, amputated at the hip. A face
evolved for that archaic torso from one organic
hint of what the lopped arm
meant around a body older than its own.

The animation of the stone recalls ancestral
figures. He feels the pressure of the bones outward.
Nervous, edgy forms. A tribal rhythm. In his
helmet head the littered ground beside the garden
discloses one more shape his hands must warm
to life. The shield turns to a knife. He meets
the other, the burden of being loved.

This cycle was written in the summer of 1972, after reading extensively on
Henry Moore's sculptures. I published all of the poems singly in various
literary journals, but until now chose to include only "The Family Group" in
a book. — MD

2. THE WOMAN

*A sculpture of a nude covered with snow makes me feel
uncomfortable, for I identify with the physical context...*
HENRY MOORE

Here on a windy carrousel we're as alive as fates
who spin the world. That woman on the left
with slate eyes like the sea memorizes clouds. Her
hair flows back to rivers underground. What
her reclining figure said impressed the sand. Her
landscaped breasts and knees, freestanding form
dictate the scale Egyptian stillness rules.

If someone came upon this woman in the dark,
the transformations of her bones, the space
contained, would tell the hills their magnitude.
The knoblike head derives from pebbles
wind and sea reduced. Caves and cliffs repeat
her arcane track, the light's long
penetration to the unknown other side.

Draped like mountains in the crinkled skin of earth
or nude against a sky her womb
takes in, she spans the solid air of that Cycladic
zone where out and in are one.
The shelter drawings hold communion in our sleep
alone, the primitive repose of exiles
from the monumental breast.

3. THE MUSIC

Those three women winding wool may have set it
going. It came from full skeins
twined between stringed figures, the barge with
heaped-up cargo, breastbones of gulls in flight.
Bells in shaken towers made a broken
music. The shell had found an echoing rejoinder.
Ringing, the high stone fortress hollowed out
the valleys:

> *Here where wind is neither harsh nor sweet*
> *Meadowlark and gull repeat each other's cry.*

Windy breakers spun the carrousel, the sea admitted
to the reeds. What matter that those
stony women fell to monitors of codes transmitted
by our bodies? Their raveled thread
denied the click of eager scissors, made the music
richer with the high half-arch release
from shore, footwear of the dead
dropping off into turbulent water. In slow

retraction of the claws when cranes scooped down to
shift a load of gravel, I heard
bulldozers in the driftwood at the lake bottom.
The music said that it would break a freeze in three
dimensions: cold creeping up from ankles,
down from the head, boneward through skin. I knew I
had to let the music in, follow the thread.

4. THE RIDE

*...the centre of gravity lies within the base (and does not
seem to be falling over or moving off its base) and yet
having an alert dynamic tension between its parts.*

Imagination rode the terror on the terrace behind
the Time-Life Screen, its figures
turning slowly to reveal an unknown face. Alert
before the aspects of that archaic rock, its
shifting triads of relation on a constant base, I
hoped to guess what moved them, the tension
of their limbs. Unlike those women who have always

loved the shape of horses, I preferred the bench.
The cracked melodeon wheezed by. The world got on
and left me drenched in sweat, afraid
to mount. I had prepared myself for flight. For fear
and pain. Until the day I saw the white
stallion with the wild blue mane. Blue, the color of
reflection. Of imagination. Of the sky. I began to

test the stirrups. Wish tight reins would fly and
move me to a sculptural conclusion larger
than my life. That shadow child, frightened, who rode
between us, eyes bluer than a blade,
grew to the shape your hands made on my shoulder. Your
music in my hair. Your heartbeat waking
in my sleeping body within the terrible air.

5. THE CHILD

He would not stay confined in that maternal arch,
the knee drawn up, a kind of looming leg
or seaside cliff to overhang the child. Although
they willed the space, to be allied
to that third form required some distortion.
The skull's complete design did not allow for change.
They passed the burden to the child, whose head,

conceived as mask, denied proportion. A shell
derived from skin and muscle, peeled off the bone.
The child lived inside. They wanted to own
a site enriched by chance occurrences: weeds,
sunlight and shade, branches falling on the terrace.
Poking among rocks, they made precise wind studies
along the shore, learned to locate shelters in the lee

of windrows. Roofs reinforced the pitch and slope of
hills, calm zones ten times the height
of trees. Controlled burning of litter on the forest
floor fertilized the choked-out
understory of fern and rhododendron. And still
the child would not come in. Waxen
as mock orange, he refused his name, the only one
they'd given: child of the place of skulls.

6. THE FAMILY GROUP

That Sunday at the zoo I understood the child
I never had would look like this: stiff-fingered
spastic hands, a steady drool, and eyes in cages
with a danger sign. I felt like stone myself,
the ancient line curved inward in a sunblind
stare. My eyes were flat. Flat eyes for tanned
young couples with their picture-story kids.

Heads turned our way but you'd learned not to care.
You stood tall as Greek columns, weather-streaked
face bent toward the boy. I wanted to take his hand,
hallucinate a husband. He whimpered at my touch.
You watched me move away and grabbed my other
hand as much in love as pity for our land-
locked town. I heard the visionary rumor of the sea.

What holds the three of us together in my mind
is something no one planned. The chiseled look of mutes.
A window shut to keep out pain. Wooden blank
of doors. That stance the mallet might surprise if it
could strike the words we hoard for fears galloping
at night over moors through convoluted bone.
The strange uncertain rumor of the sea.

I mean by sculpture what is done by main force of cutting off.

MICHELANGELO

Toward the end revolving figures slackened, came to rest
near the still center. She reviewed the pure
outline, a certain method of drawing, tried to store
a single figure in her openwork breast and head.
The light was always wrong. He could not say for sure
what they had hoped to cling to
under the rockweed web of blanket. Or where their

hooded eyes traveled on lengthening crow's-feet after
night had shut them. It may have been the first hard
opening through stone the dreamer
calls a revelation. Or the natural sun observant of
their attitudes on the floor of the great
stone quarry near Querceta where the ocean tunnels in.

Waves hollowed a threshold for that thin, upright
figure, elbows bent to support
the head. Space moved in to complement the torso, fine
articulation of the joints. But who are these
four grey sleepers, mouths open in chalky air to
the wash of winding down? Is it effigies they look for
in inky faces aging toward night?

About the Author

Spectral Waves is Madeline DeFrees's eighth full-length collection. Her *Blue Dusk: New & Selected Poems, 1951–2001* (Copper Canyon Press, 2001) won the Academy of American Poets Lenore Marshall Prize and the Washington State Book Award. She has also published short stories, essays, journalism feature stories, and two poetry chapbooks, as well as two memoirs of her nearly thirty-eight years as a nun.

DeFrees's work has been recognized by a Guggenheim Poetry Fellowship, a National Endowment for the Arts grant, and the Denise Levertov Award from *Image: A Journal of the Arts & Religion* and the Department of English of Seattle Pacific University.

DeFrees has taught at Holy Names College (renamed Fort Wright College), Spokane; the University of Montana, Missoula; and the University of Massachusetts, Amherst. She lives in Seattle and teaches in the Pacific University Low-residency M.F.A. Program.

*Copper Canyon Press wishes to acknowledge the support of
Lannan Foundation in funding the publication and distribution
of exceptional literary works.*

LANNAN LITERARY SELECTIONS 2006

Taha Muhammad Ali, *So What: New & Selected Poems*

Madeline DeFrees, *Spectral Waves*

Theodore Roethke, *Straw for the Fire:
From the Notebooks of Theodore Roethke*

Benjamin Alire Sáenz, *Dreaming the End of War*

Matthew Zapruder, *The Pajamaist*

LANNAN LITERARY SELECTIONS 2000–2005

Marvin Bell, *Rampant*

Hayden Carruth, *Doctor Jazz*

Cyrus Cassells, *More Than Peace
and Cypresses*

Norman Dubie, *The Mercy Seat:
Collected & New Poems, 1967–2001*

Sascha Feinstein, *Misterioso*

James Galvin, *X: Poems*

Jim Harrison, *The Shape of the Journey:
New and Collected Poems*

Hồ Xuân Hương, *Spring Essence:
The Poetry of Hồ Xuân Hương,* translated
by John Balaban

June Jordan, *Directed by Desire:
The Collected Poems of June Jordan*

Maxine Kumin, *Always Beginning:
Essays on a Life in Poetry*

Ben Lerner, *The Lichtenberg Figures*

Antonio Machado, *Border of a Dream:
Selected Poems,* translated by
Willis Barnstone

W.S. Merwin, *The First Four Books
of Poems, Migration: New & Selected Poems,
Present Company*

Pablo Neruda, *The Separate Rose,
Still Another Day,* translated by
William O'Daly

Cesare Pavese, *Disaffections: Complete Poems
1930–1950,* translated by Geoffrey Brock

Antonio Porchia, *Voices,* translated
by W.S. Merwin

Kenneth Rexroth, *The Complete Poems of
Kenneth Rexroth*

Alberto Ríos, *The Smallest Muscle in the
Human Body, The Theater of Night*

Theodore Roethke, *On Poetry & Craft:
Selected Prose of Theodore Roethke*

Ann Stanford, *Holding Our Own:
The Selected Poems of Ann Stanford*

Ruth Stone, *In the Next Galaxy*

Joseph Stroud, *Country of Light*

Rabindranath Tagore, *The Lover of God,*
translated by Tony K. Stewart and
Chase Twichell

*Reversible Monuments: Contemporary
Mexican Poetry,* edited by Mónica de la
Torre and Michael Wiegers

César Vallejo, *The Black Heralds,* translated
by Rebecca Seiferle

Eleanor Rand Wilner, *The Girl with Bees in
Her Hair*

C.D. Wright, *Steal Away: Selected and
New Poems*

The Chinese character for poetry is made up of two parts: "word" and "temple." It also serves as pressmark for Copper Canyon Press. Founded in 1972, Copper Canyon Press remains dedicated to publishing poetry exclusively, from Nobel laureates to new and emerging authors. The Press thrives with the generous patronage of readers, writers, booksellers, librarians, teachers, students, and funders—everyone who shares the conviction that poetry invigorates the language and sharpens our appreciation of the world.

Major funding has been provided by:

Anonymous (2)

The Paul G. Allen Family Foundation

Lannan Foundation

National Endowment for the Arts

Washington State Arts Commission

Copper Canyon Press gratefully acknowledges Mimi Gates for her generous Annual Fund support.

For information and catalogs:

COPPER CANYON PRESS
Post Office Box 271
Port Townsend, Washington 98368
360-385-4925
www.coppercanyonpress.org

The text is set in Janson Text. Janson is based on the typeface created while Hungarian traveling scholar Miklós Kis worked in Anton Janson's Amsterdam workshop in the 1680s. Adrian Frutiger and others at Linotype contributed to this 1985 digital version. The titles are set in MVB Sirenne, by Alan Dague-Greene and Mark van Bronkhorst. Sirenne was inspired by engraved captions from a 1719 natural history. Book design by Valerie Brewster, Scribe Typography. Printed on archival-quality Glatfelter Author's Text at McNaughton & Gunn.